MW00978508

This Notebook Belongs To

Molly

Made in the USA
Columbia, SC
03 August 2020

15311248R00074